AN OBAMA ODYSSEY

44

AN OBAMA ODYSSEY

Trafford rev. 05/07/2015

www.trafford.com
North America & international
toll-free: 1 888 232 4444 (USA & Canada)
fax: 812 355 4082

A DEDICATION

Far from home … undervalued and stranded
Scores of years … justice was delayed
Physically … and mentally branded
By 'friend' and foe … they were betrayed

Vile departures … through 'gates of no return'
Each … an unwilling immigrant
Heroes … 'cheek turning' … they could never learn
Accused … known to be innocent

After so long … came a glimmer of hope
The never expected … occurred
For each citizen … an expanded scope
Now perhaps … fewer dreams … deferred

For: Each generation of ancestors (yours and mine), Atieno, Hanani, Aunt Dot, Clarence & Shirley Brown, Robin & Thomas Gilliam, Rainette Holimon, Albert Jenkins, Robert Jones, Wilma Marshall King, Clemal Marthello, Lawrence McReynolds, Curtis Paradise, Doris & Sarge Stewart, Dorian Walden, Richard & Edna Washington, Louis Watts

CONTENTS

Chapter One

The Captain's Ship And Crew

The Captain and crew … under scrutiny
Their every move … I will 'check'
So against them … why would I 'mutiny'?
If somehow … they earn my respect

New Kid On The Block

From Illinois … a new kid on the 'block'
Representing … each 'contention'
A national audience … he would 'shock'
At the democrat's … convention

He seems to have … a uniting appeal
And a 'bright' … political 'tie'
With his smartness … and oratory zeal
He will 'soar' … who can tell how 'high'?

None deemed him … 'seditious' or 'sinister'
None … did 'patriotism' gnaw
Not yet 'linked' … to a 'fiery minister'
Though some were searching … for a 'flaw'

He favors … 'bi partisan seminar'
As a senator … he would 'build'
Later to be 'linked' … to the 'scimitar'
Before his ambition … was 'filled'

And so … without any hesitancy
While adhering … to his own 'tune'
Barack challenged … for the presidency
Although many … thought 'it' too soon

Kweku

Crew members … volunteered for the long haul
More were added … along the 'route'

A 'change mantra' … they 'signed on' to 'install'
That's the course … on which they'd 'recruit'

(An Obama 'Ship'?)

The crew ... an eclectic coalition?
Every 'state' ... within its range

On the status quo ... a prohibition
A crew ... dedicated to change

Captain, Crew And Ship

The crew ... an eclectic coalition
Every state ... within its range
On the status quo ... a prohibition
A crew ... dedicated to change

Crew members ... volunteered for the long haul
More were added ... along the 'route'
A 'change mantra' ... they 'signed on' to 'install'
That's the course ... on which they'd 'recruit'

The leader ... never captained such a ship
Some doubted ... that he had the heart
He knew it would be ... a hazardous trip
But such a route ... he had to 'chart'

Some thought the ship's hue ... too heavily blue
And it leaned ... too far to the left
But shades of red ... the captain would 'pursue'
In moderate seas ... he was deft

At last ... the odyssey was set to start
From course ... the crew would not sever
The captain ... was charismatic and smart
Forward ever ... backward never

Kweku

Elephant Opposition

The 'Obama Ship' ... some chose to malign
Of steadiness ... they were wary
Some challenged the 'strength' ... of the 'ship design'
No 'elephants' ... could it 'carry'

They thought the hull ... was badly neglected
Design ... they continued to note
The 'platform' ... they completely rejected
Not one believed ... the ship would 'float'

Barack was too 'liberal' ... with the 'paint'
The 'helm' ... was difficult to steer
Replies from Barack's crew ... were never 'faint'
They retorted ... 'hope over fear'

Building a ship ... difficult and massive
It's quite ... an enormous pursuit
With a captain ... deemed timid and passive
'Donkey ships' ... 'Elephants' refute

Kweku

Recognition List

To be expected … vile hostile morass
Some to 'truth stretching' … will relate
Gross innuendo … designed to harass
Barack's election … to negate

Appeal to the hopeful … he must measure
With fear mongers … time must be brief
To democrats … electable treasure
For republicans … constant grief

With 'blue donkeys' … he must keep his 'ship' full
'Red elephants' … he must pursue
Will a blue and red 'crew' … have enough 'pull'?
To stage … a political coup

Each primary … will add to genesis
With his 'allies' … he must compete
Nomination … will bring his nemesis
The 'big elephant' … to 'defeat'

Kweku

Despite Obama's ... 'blue fleet' potential
Quite difficult ... will be his 'sail'

A 'blue and red fleet' ... will be essential
If his voyage ... is to prevail

To prevent … a republican 'repeat'
And a presidency … attain

JOHN McCAIN
THE REPUBLICAN
BIG RED ELEPHANT
CIRCA 2008

The 'Big Elephant' … Barack must defeat
'Reincarnated' … John McCain

I ... The People

Will I help ... to 'make' a new president?
As I gauge... each non congruence
In my support ... I won't be hesitant
If in views ... I find confluence

A cabinet post ... will not be my fate
On such a list ... I won't be 'high'
But my candidate ... is not an ingrate
A post offered ... I would deny

I will not ... leave my candidate alone
In solitary ... perdition
I will be the power ... behind his 'throne'
Empowered ... without 'position'

Barack Hussein Obama ... 'tops' my 'list'
As the candidate ... of my choice
On Barack Obama ... I must insist
I hope through him ... to have a 'voice'

Kweku

Inclusive

Barack 'knows' ... on him it is conducive
Each citizen ... he must pursue
And so his team ... he has made inclusive
To reflect the red ... white and blue

For Obama's team ... no 'prohibition'
In non exclusion ... a 'high zeal'
His team ... is an open coalition
Of the American ... 'ideal'

Educated ... unlearned ... the young and old
Colors ... of the human 'rainbow'
The rich ... the poor ... with the shy and the bold
Each 'yes we can' ... who 'disdains 'no'

All those ... who see the past as a 'fossil'
And choose to replace fear ... with hope
'Beyond race' and 'gender' ... the non 'docile'
Those who hand the struggling ... a 'rope'

People who protest ... for the innocent
And each 'underdog' ... they have 'backed'
Those who recognize ... what is imminent
With such ... his voting claque is 'stacked'

Kweku

11

Obama Drama

The son-in-law said … that he backed Clinton
His 'outburst' … was meant as a 'joke'
And for the 'outburst' … he was 'repentant'
When father-in-law … seemed to 'choke'

'Ayaye jowa' … his dad-in-law shrieked
Venting … his Luo emotion
Had his son's in law brains … in some way 'leaked'?
And damaged … his voting 'notion'

Words from his son in law … had brought him grief
Still Obama … he would endorse
That his son in law joked … brought him 'relief'
But no stronger … could be his 'choice'

His son-in-law … lives in the USA
A citizen … able to vote
He feels certain … he will vote the 'right way'
In a manner … that he can 'gloat'

My theory … on no study relied
But I guarantee it … as 'fact'
Could Kenyans vote … it would be a 'landslide'
One candidate … Kenyans 'impact'

Should each Kenyan vote … in the USA
There would be … so little drama
One candidate would win … 'going away'
It would be … Barack Obama

Kweku

12

Foreign Aid

The phone calls were 'thoughtful' … long and sundry
But in many ways … all the same
For Obama 'facts' … callers were 'hungry'
Obama … each caller would 'claim'

As a socialist … Barack was accused
An Arab … and a Muslim too
Phony charges … that each caller defused
With **my** vote … **they** knew what to do

Obama was thought … a 'foreign agent'
A 'fact' … each caller would protest
They deemed such charges … as lies and 'flagrant'
Their feelings … each caller 'confessed'

Calls from Kenya … Ghana … Germany too
Callers saw news … on 'CNN'
On the phone … their enthusiasm grew
Barack Obama … had to 'win'

They 'demanded' … that I 'represent' them
In the way … that I cast my vote
Their advocacy … spilled over the brim
Barack … they were quick to promote

Their 'advice' to me … was not trivial
It seemed through me … their voices 'spoke'
Each 'suggestion' … was unequivocal
For Obama … I had to vote

Kweku

13

Chapter Two

Charting The Waters

Through uncharted waters … the ship will sail
To some areas … unexplored
Through the unknown … can Obama prevail?
Will U. S. prestige … be restored?

Charting The Waters

To 'communities' … he would 'minister'
As lawyer … and as teacher too
First 'state' … then United States Senator
For him … there was more to pursue

To 'commonality' … amenable
Let 'difference' … take a 'back seat'
'Disagree' … don't be 'disagreeable'
Concepts … he has chosen to 'fete'

Red … white … and blue … he opted to endorse
Each color … a part of the whole
That was the 'oneness' … he chose to 'enforce'
The presidency … is his goal

February 10th … 2007
Spouting … *in unity we share*
With a 'beginning' … he hoped would 'leaven'
For president … he did declare

For such a 'run' … he was more than content
And he chose … to announce that day
No move made … was without Michelle's 'consent'
Then his campaign … was on its way

From city to city … his voice grew hoarse
Old politics … he seemed to dread
Despite each trammel … he would stay on 'course'
His message … he wanted to spread

Kweku

16

The First Course

'Growth' now much more ... than a 'conversation'
To each democrat ... quite well known
He directs each move ... toward nomination
The gauntlet ... Obama has 'thrown'

Already spouting ... his 'change' proponent
With 'win' ... glistening in each eye
Hillary ... is his major opponent
But no other ... will he deny

Through uncharted waters ... the trip will lead
To some areas ... unexplored
Through the unknown ... can Obama succeed?
Will U. S. prestige ... be restored?

Kweku

Nomination Critique

When Hillary … decided to concede
'Success' v 'failure' … did prevail
It was seldom … how did Barack succeed?
But rather … how did Clinton fail?

A debate … did pundits try to 'invite'
Unanswered 'questions' … to prolong
Not … how did Barack Obama … go 'right'?
But … how did Hillary … go 'wrong'?

The 'answers' … pundits may appear to seek
Without 'checking' … 'answer places'
Perhaps … in 'their' 'nomination critique'
They did not 'touch' … all the 'bases'

Kweku

Change Of Course

Applause for Barack ... cheerful yet raucous
Kudos ... among his crew were 'tossed'
Obama won ... the Iowa caucus
New Hampshire's primary ... he 'lost'

Despite New Hampshire ... 'lead domination'
Finally ... insurmountable
Obama would win ... the nomination
And vowed to be ... accountable

'Democratic nomination ... refrain'
General election ... to go
The 'ship's direction' veered ... toward John McCain
Obama's ... republican foe

Kweku

Winding Down

Through 'primary winds' … Barack's ship 'sailed strong'
Much stronger … than was purported
Many thought 'Barack's direction' … was 'wrong'
Since Hillary … they supported

Both party conventions … have come and gone
To V. P. candidates … some 'turn'
Barack and McCain … no longer 'alone'
Biden … Palin … 'assets' to 'learn'

There were voters … that Barack did not 'reach'
For some … a favorite spiel
Barack … with those voters … had a huge 'breach'
Incumbent … on Barack to 'heal'

Each pundit … named that particular 'bloc'
Without any … hesitancy
'Blue collar' whites … would bolster Barack's 'stock'
For the U. S. … presidency

Drawing near … the general election
Primary days … at last long past
For some … elation … others … dejection
November 4th … approaching 'fast'

On history … two men are encroaching
A role … neither has seen before
The presidency … 'one' is approaching
Is Barack … 'number forty four'?

Kweku

Chapter Three

Rough Weather

Polls picking Barack ... seem to 'vacillate'
But my prayers ... for Barack are strong
Me ... one reality ... does fascinate
There are still 'things' ... that can go wrong

(Bad Weather Brewing)

Journeys … are not always uneventful
The 'breeze' … 'sea' … 'snow' or 'sand' … may shift

While at such 'turns' … one may be 'resentful'
Sometimes … one must 'roll' … with the 'drift'

Radar Screen

Innuendo ... linked to Obama's name
While awaiting ... the 'right moment'
Facts distorted ... and aiming to defame
To the 'willing' ... more than cogent

His foes ... will Obama try to demean?
And make 'mountains' ... from a mole hill
Obama appears to be ... 'squeaky clean'
Vile epithets ... will his foes 'till'?

On Barack's team ... the 'antennas' 'went up'
And created ... a radar screen
Will Barack's candidacy ... some 'disrupt'?
Much more than likely ... such did seem

Kweku

Campaign Obama

His genetic background ... has been portrayed
Father ... Kenyan ... his mother ... white
As the 'change candidate' ... he is 'parlayed'
So symbolic ... of what is 'right'

For 'president' ... an unlike applicant
Not ... in the Jesse Jackson 'spin'
Obama is not ... a 'black aspirant'
As Jackson ... and Sharpton have been

Such rhetoric ... media promoted
Their 'innocuous' ... hint at race
'They' say ... in no way was race denoted
Not even ... with the slightest 'trace'

Many say that 'race talk' ... promotes tension
A subject ... they seek to avoid
But now in the news ... more than a 'mention'
And some ... seem to be ... overjoyed

The catalyst ... has been Reverend Wright
The media ... is quick to 'say'
But perhaps ... that may be an 'oversight'
If 'a Clinton' ... spurred on the fray

It seems detractors talk ... with no 'comma'
Negative talk ... from dusk to dawn
Their talk is about ... Barack Obama
Still ... to the white house ... he is 'drawn'

The states Hillary won ... 'they' say he can't
Over that matter ... 'they' debate
On his 'elitism' ... they choose to rant
To 'blue collars' ... he can't relate

But his 'backers' tell ... a different tale
One ... of a high blood count ... in 'creeds'
To Barack ... 'donkeys' and 'elephants' 'pale'
Barack acts ... for the country's ... 'needs'

To get elected ... 'Obama's lure' ... lacks
He is ... a 'feel good' illusion
Some emphasize ... his appeal is to 'blacks'
Despite ... 'primary conclusions'

'Revisited' ... much more than 'now and then'
Unable ... to release the 'guard'
It's America's ... 'original sin'
Variations ... of the 'race card'

His vulnerability ... 'enlarges'
More ... of the political stink
Ayers and Rezko ... corruption charges
To each one ... an attempted 'link'

Approaching 'home' ... wanting a win dearly
Declarations ... are now more rough
Hillary chooses ... to state quite clearly
Obama ... is not tough enough

Iraq War ... economy ... gas prices
Are every voter's ... concern
Is Obama ... strongest ... in a 'crisis'?
Other 'hopefuls' ... will voters 'spurn'?

A huge issue ... the rising health care 'rate'
Hillary ... versus ... Obama
Both campaigned 'hard' ... for a primary 'fate'
Debates brought ... suspense and drama

He and wife Michelle ... have both been 'inferred'
Citizens ... unpatriotic
The media's wrath ... they have both incurred
In a manner ... vitriolic

Obama ... says race won't be a factor
Media members ... disagree
Will Obama ... be a 'race redactor'?
As to race ... does he have the 'key'?

Kweku

The Obama Suite

There are false accusations ... some explore
On the basest thoughts ... many 'prey'
Each accusation ... detractors 'encore'
Lies that the truth ... cannot allay

Sometimes it's 'war' ... other times 'politics'
A possible ... destructive 'end'
Both may result ... in the 'apocalypse'
Able to destroy ... foe or friend

Of such things ... the 'defense' must be alert
To aspersions ... they cannot yield
Any attack ... they must try to divert
Each accusation ... they must 'field'

Part and parcel ... of the 'Obama Suite'
'Field' each lie ... however 'farfetched'
Often idiotic ... never discrete
Through a vile mind ... such lies are 'sketched'

Kweku

An Unpatriotic Pair

Michelle was buoyed … by Obama's campaign
A good feeling … it did provoke
But the words she chose … would cause some disdain
A 'back lash' … her words did promote

She … for the first time … proud of her country
The conservatives … were aghast
Condemnation … was direct … and sundry
Unpatriotic … she was 'cast'

The 'pledge of allegiance' … Barack won't say
The U. S. … he aims to destroy
A 'Muslim terrorist' … his 'secret play'
The presidency … just a ploy

At Michelle and Barack … detractors 'stare'
On … 'no they can't' … the cynics 'rest'
They are dubbed … 'an unpatriotic pair'
Though … to 'yes WE can' … they attest

Kweku

28

(The Enemy Within?)

Obama and wife … came under 'attack'
Another … sought them … to pester

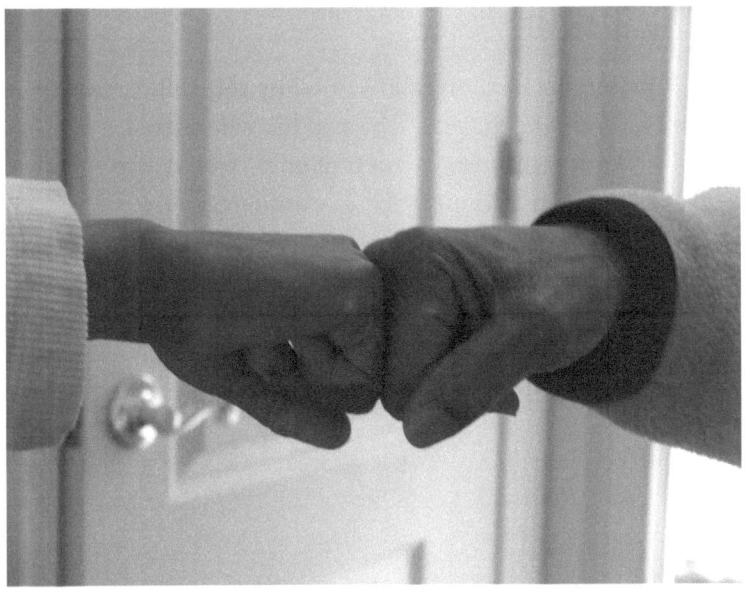

Obama's armor … a man tried to 'crack'
For what seemed … a 'fist pump' … gesture
(A 'TERRORIST' PUMP?)

The Fist Pump

While seeking ... 'delegate domination'
Barack ... would get over the 'hump'
Joy spread ... when he clinched the nomination
For Michelle and him ... a 'fist pump'

Obama and wife ... came under 'attack'
Another ... sought them ... to pester
Obama's armor ... a man tried to 'crack'
For what seemed ... a 'fist pump' ... gesture

A fist pump ... soon followed ... by the 'thumbs up'
Were the moves ... he and his wife shared
On one gesture ... a detractor ... would 'sup'
A base analysis ... was 'bared'

He labeled their 'moves' ... a 'terrorist pump'
A totally ... different 'slant'
In his 'thought processes' ... was there a 'slump'?
Or just a 'work ... related' rant

Kweku

The Joke

As to assassinating … 'Osama'
She suggested … somebody would
And then she 'substituted' … Obama
To 'get' both of them … if they could

Was it … 'political machination'?
Sparked by words … that one person 'spoke'
Barack Obama's … assassination?
That she said … was merely a joke

Kweku

Whitey

A 'label' for whites ... Michelle had 'planted'
She spoke ... at Reverend Wright's church
From his pulpit ... 'Whitey' ... she had 'ranted'
For proof ... no one would have to 'search'

A radio host ... 'thickened' the malaise
And from him ... she could not escape
There was no objection ... that she could 'raise'
Since the video ... was on 'tape'

Not true ... the 'Obama Camp' would reply
There is no tape ... that can 'exist'
How ... can a right thinking person ... deny?
That on nonsense ... some foes insist

Kweku

Barack's Baby Mama

Campaigns … are alleged to be … 'color blind'
Without a negative … on race
Yet there are some things … that seem … 'well designed'
And of race … there's at least a 'trace'

For Michelle … a nonsensical rumor
Filled … with 'procreation drama'
An accusation … devoid of humor
Cast as Barack's … 'baby mama'

Kweku

Political Muck

That Joe Biden … was known to 'over blurt'
A reputation … he had earned
His own 'addendum' … he chose to 'insert'
Some say at that … democrats 'burned'

Sarah Palin … was never thought a snob
Many republicans … liked her
Others called her a 'diva' … and 'whack job'
An 'in house squabble' … to deter

The campaign rhetoric … many noted
And each Obama 'charge' … was grim
In 'spreading the wealth' … Karl Marx was quoted
But fingers were pointed … at 'him'

Through all of that … Obama took the heat
His emotions … remained intact
Obama linked McCain … to the 'Bush seat'
And to that … voters … did react

A maverick and 'fighter' … well tested
Republican … adulation
McCain … 8 years with George Bush 'invested'
Democratic … allegation

Inconsistent … with thoughts that soon 'scatter'
John's judgment … was deemed 'sporadic'
Obama's team 'pounded' … on that 'matter'
And dubbed John McCain … 'erratic'

John said … experience was essential
Barack's judgment … 'weighed' unsteady
For 'rock crowds' … Barack may have potential
But for president … unready

John McCain's 'leadership' … instigated
Loads of 'kill the terrorist' … muck
Just a few crazies … were implicated
Sarah Palin … 'ran with the 'buck'

Unpatriotic … Barack and his wife
To the 'left' … positioned too far
From the 'right' … snide accusations were rife
'Right wing' behavior … that seemed 'par'

To the conservatives … 'one' brings delight
Labeled … a racist minister
He is Reverend … Jeremiah Wright
'Linked' to Barack … and sinister

Each the other … would try to agitate
About charges … both would complain
One … the skinheads sought … to assassinate
Barack Obama … not McCain

To prove him terror_ist_ … some may still try
Social_ist_ charges … may not end
To make him elit_ist_ … some may still vie
Though none of those '_ists_' … has he been

Kweku

Political Falderal

The age qualification … 'satisfied'
But 'natural born' … some deny
The residency part … 'unverified'
As to his mother … some decry

Mombasa Kenya … as his place of birth
There are litigants … who lay 'claim'
Not qualified … for a president's 'berth'
Therefore withdraw … Obama's name

From him … 'president elect' should be 'shorn'
Old issues of his birth … arise
Questions as to where … Obama was born
A controversy … to apprise

Just falderal … by an 'opposition'
To stem … the inevitable
Half truths and lies … were no 'competition'
The vote … was irrevocable

A calm opposition … was their 'new voice'
Falderal … inconsequential
Overwhelmingly … Barack was their 'choice'
His each act … was 'presidential'

Lies crushed … by the audacity to hope
The voters … would not be 'muted'
With hope over fear … voters chose to cope
Fervor … could not be disputed

Kweku

Healthy Paranoia

On the 'vote' … paranoia has risen
For some … wanting their voices heard
An attempt to vote … could foment schism
'Counted' 'or not' … which one occurred?

Into old 'truths'… many blacks have been 'thrust'
'Future' like the past … they 'detect'
'Outsiders' shake their heads … at such 'distrust'
Blacks are 'paranoid … some 'reflect'

Charges of paranoia … give a 'key'
And so … such charges … seem to 'stick'
'Paranoia' … and 'healthy minds' 'agree'
If not 'paranoid' … blacks are 'sick'

A McCain campaigner … 'pushed the clock' back
A rape charge … on a white girl's word
The paranoid faction … of the black claque
For the worst … they began to gird

Barack's 'illegal aunt' … was 'reported'
'Similar' Kenyans … were pursued
That many … were already deported
To the 'paranoid' … was 'prelude'

Some carry 'life histories' … to the 'poll'
Their smallest fact … pre-inspected
Prayers … that votes mean 'something' … a common goal
They don't want … their votes rejected

Registration records ... purportedly 'lost'
Phone calls ... to change a voter's 'say'
By arbitrary 'demands' ... 'double crossed'
Remindful of ... 'another day'

'Pledge of Allegiance' ... 'backwards' to recite
And without ... any 'rehearsal'
Civil War between the states ... to 'refight'
'Lobbying' ... for a 'reversal'

They were aware ... such things sounded ... 'far-fetched'
Against such 'trends' ... they were 'guarded'
Deep within ... similarities were 'etched'
If dormant ... perhaps 'restarted'

They pull the lever ... Obama their choice
'Tension' ... not relief has mounted
And so for them ... it is tough to rejoice
They fear their 'vote' ... went 'uncounted'

Unable ... each 'past act' ... to 'vaccinate'
'Flooded' in minds ... memories 'seep'
Barack they fear ... 'one' will assassinate
'Saturates' their minds ... wide and 'deep'

Kweku

A Non Issue … Issue

In the campaign … a non issue is race
From race … all those 'involved' refrain
And 'of race' … should there be the slightest 'trace'
The 'righteous' … will quickly 'complain'

But some have made … a puzzling conclusion
Barack is given … too much 'slack'
So … are they propagating … 'confusion'?
'Implying' … because he is black

Kweku

Chapter Four

Land Sighted

Barack's tactics ... now seem more relevant
In his crew ... he has complete trust
He seems 'right' ... on 'wooing' the 'elephant'
And on that ... he did not adjust

Now that he 'sees' ... the 'point of arrival'
At the sight ... he is more than 'glad'
Soon an end ... to the 'punch' and 'reprisal'
The 'cruise' ... he may think 'not so bad'

'Voting poll' margins ... appear to widen
McCain and Palin ... lagging back
The polls suggest ... Obama and Biden
'The Change We Can Believe In' ... claque

Six Days Remaining

One newspaper ... had 'Barack' 'printed in'
Since their newspaper ... should be 'first'
Headlines 'blared' ... ***"A Barack Obama Win"***
For November 4th ... they 'rehearsed'

The presidency ... was still Barack's quest
By 'success' ... he was not 'seduced'
On his laurels ... Obama would not 'rest'
An 'infomercial' ... he produced

An agreement ... McCain said ... Barack signed
Public funds ... he agreed to use
Obama backed down ... and he changed his mind
McCain called ... Barack's 'pledge' a ruse

McCain says ... much too weak is Obama
Barack's inexperience ... shows
He is unable ... to catch Osama
Or any of the U. S. ... 'foes'

On Barack ... 'the right' cast another 'spin'
A 'new man' ... with a Muslim name
Barack 'meeting' with him ... a 'right wing sin'
P. L. O. 'linked' ... the right would claim

Woe for Israel ... supporters 'disdain'
A conservative ... prediction
Anti Semite 'blood' ... in Obama's 'vein'
A conservative ... depiction

Toward the 'ugly' … McCain still seemed to 'steer'
Those tactics … he would not abort
Prime on his mind … were 'politics of fear'
Perhaps it was … his last resort

Obama campaigned … for 'hope' over 'fear'
Needed change … he vowed to foment
Though Barack shifted … to a higher 'gear'
His statements … were calm and cogent

A lead … some say Barack is sustaining
'Rocking' … the 'political boat'
To election day … six days remaining
Six more days … before we can vote

Kweku

Vote Polls

I will await results ... with bated breath
On no 'vote poll' ... do I rely
My stance will not change ... not even by death
Polls always truthful ... I deny

What the voters 'say' ... before election
I cannot ... readily believe
What voters 'say' ... may require 'inspection'
Their intent may be ... to deceive

'Vote polls' pick 'winners' ... before voters vote
'Winners' ... polls don't always ... 'project'
Over poll results ... candidates may gloat
Polls ... not picking them ... they 'reject'

'Honest' responses ... leave no mystery
But words of 'truth' ... voters ... may 'cloak'
And should I recall ... voter history
Sometimes 'true votes' ... the polls revoke

Truman v Dewey ... vote tallies ... would 'stun'
And Dinkins ... v ... Guliani
Then Bradley's ... gubernatorial ... 'run'
Showed polls ... a 'vote ... hootenanny'

The polls 'picked' ... the wrong winner ... in each 'race'
'Pre-vote' ... were voters uncertain?
True 'inclines' ... do voters refuse ... to 'face'?
Until ... there's a 'voting curtain'

Between past and present … a great divide
The mantra … many 'pundits' 'cast'
Yet great doubt in vote polls … others 'provide'
Learned reaction … to a known 'past'

In the polls … Obama has forged ahead
Many say … he has won the fray
By the polls … others may choose to be led
I will be 'convinced' … 'voting day'

Kweku

The Last Gasp

The election … is in Obama's 'grasp'
Victory for him … some 'declared'
However McCain … retained a 'last gasp'
Some declared … his campaign 'repaired'

Now much more … of a political tier
A 'congressional … connection'
A president with congress … the 'right' fear
And seek a 'right wing' … correction

How Obama … Pelosi … Reid … 'impede'
John McCain … chooses to relate
Confident … that his message … will succeed
In November … 2008

At Barack's 'readiness' … he will still 'swipe'
Of that 'assault' … he will not 'tire'
He hopes voters … will believe the 'hype'
Obama will 'melt' … under 'fire'

In no way … is Barack a remedy
Since he lacks … proper continence
Obama is 'soft' … on the 'enemy'
In him … none should have confidence

Barack's flag pin 'trauma' … somehow 'dwindled'
Arguments had grown … somewhat trite
An old 'itch' … the GOP 'rekindled'
Reverend … Jeremiah … Wright

Obama is risky … and radical
Again … the GOP refrain
As president … he will be 'prodigal'
McCain … continues to 'maintain'

Barack concedes … the race is not over
And still connects … McCain with Bush
He does not expect … a 'four leaf clover'
For votes … he continues to 'push'

Kweku

(Unbwogable Like Barack)

Threats … innuendoes … lies … his portrayal
His character probed … to condemn

But Barack's fortitude … seems to prevail
Since nobody … can 'bwogo' him

Unbwogable

In morality ... he is 'derelict'
His associations ... bring guilt
Barack is a Muslim ... and 'terrorist'
The direction ... some try to 'tilt'

Some label him ... as a 'foreign agent'
Elitist ... not to be believed
But Obama remains ... cool and patient
He ... presidential ... some perceived

Himself ... from no truth ... did Barack perjure
At no time ... was he hesitant
A Kenyan ... and American 'merger'
Is he to be ... the president?

From his father's Luo ... the Kenyan side
One tribal word ... makes some things 'clear'
'Bwoga' ... in some ways ... may be used to chide
To bwoga ... is ... to instill 'fear'

English prefix ... and suffix ... add 'power'
'Un' ... and 'able' ... merge with the word
'Unbwogable' ... suggests ...one won't cower
Unbwogable Barack ... inferred

Threats ... innuendoes ... lies ... his portrayal
His character probed ... to condemn
Obama's fortitude ... seems to prevail
Since nobody ... can 'bwogo' him

Kweku

49

November 5th

So long ago set ... was one precedent
Evident ... and easy to gauge
Never would there be ... a black president
Blacks echoed ... at every age

Never ever ... in 'my time' ... would such be
Was a significant ... black view
Few thought they would live ... long enough ... to see
A president ... with a 'like hue'

To the fifth of 'Never' ... blacks did relate
And that date ... was the consensus
An event ... never open to 'debate'
So was never ... deemed contentious

Come November 5th ... will most blacks rely?
On the 'new white house ... resident'
The 5th of 'Never' ... will blacks then deny?
'Convinced' ... by the 'new president'

Some expect ... 'heavenly intervention'
Supporting ... one candidate's 'clout'
Are there still 'reasons' ... for apprehension?
In the process ... is there still doubt?

Will voters produce ... a uniting 'scene'?
Illuminating ... the drama
Will Senator McCain's ... concession ... 'mean'?
President ... Barack ... Obama

Kweku

50

The Day After

Quite a bit different ... was 'yesterday'
That was before ... the 'change of guard'
Different rhetoric ... then on display
Labeled ... the 'republican card'

Black democrats ... republicans would chide
While displaying ... their 'lofty bait'
One fact ... republicans chose not ... to 'hide'
Two black ... Secretaries of State

Democrat ... how can any black remain?
For 'high appointments' ... blacks must wait
Loyalty to democrats ... seems arcane
With 'republicans' ... blacks should 'mate'

Did yesterday ... 'bring' a 'black president'?
Does the 'old bait' ... seem more 'brittle'?
Is the G. O. P. ... now more reticent?
'Secretaries' ... seem so 'little'

On the horizon ... a new era 'turns'
A change in 'batons' ... to be 'twirled'
McCain's candidacy ... no longer 'churns'
Barack is leader ... of the world

'Today' ... is there 'terroristic concern?
Did the 'fist pump' ... create a 'bump'?
Or in unison ... does the country 'turn'?
To aid the 'domestic ... gas pump'

Oil crisis ... gas prices ... economy
Includes ... the weakening dollar
The 'elitist' ... and the ecology
Issues ... for Barack to 'collar'

Will 'Obama foes' ... elect to 'duel'?
For what he does ... or does not do
Should Barack 'find' ... alternative fuel
Perhaps rapprochement ... will ensue

In North Korea ... Iraq ... and Iran
Every ... 'axis of evil'
Somewhere ... between diplomacy ... and 'brawn'
Barack's response ... can't be 'feeble'

Will there be ... an 'increase' in 'systolic'?
Another ... 'he was the first' stat
Will his election ... surpass 'symbolic'?
Despite ... so little time for 'that'

Will Obama's win ... quickly 'influence'?
The 'ways' ... in which people behave
Will the 'N word' ... with every nuance?
Become an expression ... to 'shave'

When necessary ... will black and white 'talk'?
In a manner ... that's quite sincere
At an issue ... will 'either' choose ... to 'balk'?
Will 'one' the 'other' ... 'lend an ear'?

Will talk be as though ... 'one' does not exist?
Will the presence of 'both' ... be felt?
On a 'stacked deck' ... will either side insist?
From the 'top' ... will each 'card' get dealt?

Again in reverie … I have been 'caught'
I assumed … Barack's election
I ask … was all my writing … just for 'naught'?
An 'afterthought' … of dejection

Perhaps … I should define … 'the day after'
November 5th … 2008
That day … did I manufacture … 'laughter'?
Did I learn … I still have to 'wait'?

Kweku

Perhaps

The course was charted … the crew selected
There were 'rough seas' … along the way
The turbulence … was surely expected
Success is not … served on a tray

Barack … and winning … irrevocable
A truly … strong … correlation
President … Barack … inevitable?
Perhaps … divine … coronation

Kweku

Chapter Five

President Elect

Outcome speculation … was copious
The ups and downs … of the campaign
So many had fear … of the 'odious'
Now there is joy … they can't contain

Barack Obama … has finally won
A 'healthy' margin … evident
A new mantle … will the democrat 'don'?
As 'non partisan … president'

With final 'projections' … some could connect
But I … didn't think 'it' … a cinch
When Barack became … 'President Elect'
Myself … I was compelled … to pinch

All my thoughts … I prematurely 'condensed'
The impact on me … still not clear
When … of the announcement … I was convinced
There may have been … trace … of a tear

(November 4, 2008 ~8 P. M. Est)

They voted 'Barack' ... what could they then do?
While awaiting ... the 'final count'

Each 'butterfly stomach' ... left a known clue
Tension within ... began to mount

A Growing Dream

To him ... constant dreaming ... his 'malady'
And each dream ... seemed to end ... the same
Each dream was 'real' ... not one ... a 'fallacy'
He the 'hero' ... in any 'game'

Academic ... and athletic success
Each one ... to presage his future
One dream the next one ... would always buttress
No dream ... did he choose to 'suture'

Company president ... or CEO
The captain ... of the football team
Every dream ... made his ambition 'grow'
Reality ... each dream did seem

Euphoria ... seemed to be 'premature'
There were trammels ... blocking each road
His success ... at 'best' ... seemed to be 'obscure'
Linked ... to a segregation code

But by falderal ... he was not deterred
He worked hard ... like any other
Was it true his dream ... had to be deferred?
But might apply ... to another

Company president ... and CEO
Both positions ... his 'new dreams' 'veil'
To the 'top' of the 'pole' ... his dreams now go
U. S. presidency ... to 'scale'

The 'mountain top' ... each dream ... appears to 'say'
The 'national scene' ... lends drama
But today ... he dreams each dream ... all the way
'President ... Barack Obama'

Kweku

One Base

Up in the morning ... eager not surly
With an agenda ... to promote
Defying ... blacks will not ... wake up 'early'
Especially ... when it's to vote

But quite early ... on one day ... blacks did 'rise'
Stood in long lines ... hour after hour
While their 'voting bent' ... offered ... no surprise
They hoped their vote ... foretold power

Early that day ... they ... volunteers would 'court'
And that 'base' ... was not reticent
The Obama 'camp' ... they vowed ... to support
They helped make ... a new president

Kweku

(Beginning Of A Long Journey)

The Obama team … had devised a 'scheme'
How the 'highest mountain' … they'd 'scale'

(To A Residence Thought Unreachable)

THE WHITE HOUSE

What some saw ... as an impossible dream
At least one thought ... a fairy tale

An Impossible Dream

The Obama team … had devised a 'scheme'
How the 'highest mountain' … they'd 'scale'
What some saw … as an impossible dream
At least one thought … a fairy tale

Plans … to make a president … were conceived
Democratic will … would 'regroup'
Obama's election … they … had 'perceived'
A nation's prestige … to 'recoup'

Expecting the night … to recognize him
For that moment … Barack prepared
November 4th … at 11 p. m.
A new … president … was 'declared'

Kweku

The Answer

For some ... Barack had 'a pied piper's lure'
His message ... they seemed to 'swallow'
'Things' that were ... they wanted not ... to endure
Obama ... they chose to follow

Any ... who were in 'darkness' ... or 'despair'
Barack promised them ... 'light' and 'hope'
He said ... *of the old ways ... they should beware*
Choose change that we need ... with your vote

When Obama ... spoke of *change that we need*
Voters saw themselves ... part of 'we'
Then Barack's message ... they began to 'heed'
With him ... they began to agree

Democracy ... voters put in motion
Voting day ... was their day to 'move'
To them ... the vote was a potent potion
Barack ... 'the answer' ... votes would 'prove'

Kweku

An Obama Odyssey

To the senate … Barack was somewhat 'new'
Yet he thought … that he could do more
A higher office … he sought to pursue
President … number forty four

On his ambition … he was not timid
He was filled … with tremendous hope
Barack saw only … the sky his limit
So … with his new view … he would 'cope'

Barack and his team … were underrated
Unexpected … was his 'ascent'
But their efforts … never 'undulated'
Clear early on … was their intent

No 'old politics' … was his decision
'Civil' … his campaign was to be
He would 'fight' … 'politics of division'
'Inclusion' … all voters would 'see'

Despite … his character devastation
His mantra … was hope over fear
The white house … was his planned 'destination'
To a 'straight path' … he would adhere

Some looked at his run … as an 'oddity'
Under their radar … just for 'fun'
It became … an Obama Odyssey
He would make … a successful 'run'

With each primary debate ... he would 'grow'
It was 'campaign heat' ... some 'reasoned'
To 'higher heights' ... he was ready to 'go'
The 'heat' had made him ... more 'seasoned'

Barack's ... Iowa primary success
Iowa voters ... had their 'say'
Still to come ... more political duress
More new 'drama' ... was on the way

'Trammels' ... seemed 'torpedoes' ... in his 'ship lane'
Ayers ... Rezko ... and Wright ... distractions
An alleged ... P ... L ... O 'link' ... a 'new bane'
Charges ... from opposing ... 'factions'

Barack the 'Arab terrorist' ... was 'cast'
With a socialist Marxist ... 'bent'
His 'opponents' tried to make ... charges 'last'
To derail his lofty ... 'ascent'

The economy ... government 'buy out'
Crises that 'swung things' ... Barack's 'way'
Barack would have won anyway ... no doubt
Many voters ... are prone to 'say'

In their graves ... ancestors begin to 'stir'
Now awakened ... from a long 'sleep'
With no 'dreams' ... that such would ever 'occur'
'Praise' ... on each descendant ... they 'heap'

At the white house ... considerable 'change'
The house that slaves ... had helped to build
Ancestors ... may think of the change as 'strange'
With 'hue' like theirs ... the house has 'filled'

Michelle Obama … Barack's special one
The woman … he chose for his wife
Integral to each 'thing' … that he has done
His devoted … partner for life

Daughters Malia and Sasha … just two
Family moments … they now 'bare'
Every intimacy … they pursue
Now with the public … they must 'share'

The 'first family … Obamas will be
Perhaps … a different 'model'
To 'success' … should Obama have the 'key'
Then that model … we should 'bottle'

Barack has been said … to be transcendent
Beyond gender … and beyond race
With help … from each ancestor's … descendant
Any 'embargo'… he can 'face'

Kweku

(November 4, 2008 ~11 P. M. Est)

Toward celebration ... voters were behooved
Over Obama ... they would dote

It seemed that for months ... voters had been 'moved'
For Obama ... they had to vote

CELEBRATION!

Obama Wins U.S. Presidential Election!

Ghana … Germany … Kenya calls … 'came in'
Kudos … from all over … were 'hurled'

Each one … seemed to relish … in 'Barack's win'
THE 'SHOT' HEARD … ALL AROUND … THE
WORLD

President Barack Hussein Obama!

A day … most never expected … to 'see'
Or 'taste' … 'political manna'

Photograph 13

'Special' … election day … turned out to be
PRESIDENT … BARACK … OBAMA

A BEGINNING?

President Barack Obama

Euphoria had spread ... like a 'wild fire'
Pent-up emotions ... 'exploded'
'Joyous words' were like 'preaching ... to the choir'
Pride in the way ... each one voted

Men and women ... would wipe away a tear
While others ... just openly 'cried'
A schism ... between 'confidence' and 'fear'
So on hope ... each voter 'relied'

Toward celebration ... voters were behooved
Over Obama ... they would dote
It seemed that for months ... voters had been 'moved'
For Obama ... they had to vote

They had heard all the jibes ... about his name
For president ... it did not 'fit'
He ... anti American ... some would claim
Well with them ... such claims did not 'sit'

The old and young ... both openly 'confessed'
That they had voted ... from the 'heart'
And now with history ... they are 'obsessed'
Having played ... an integral part

On so many shoulders ... Obama 'stood'
A 'list' that's too long ... to mention
Before Barack ... others did what they could
Which aided ... Barack's 'ascension'

To Moses … Dr. King has been 'likened'
The 'promised land' … he did not 'gain'
But yet the people … had been 'enlightened'
Is Barack … a 'Joshua vein'?

A day … most never expected to 'see'
Or 'taste' … 'political manna'
'Special' … election day turned out to be
PRESIDENT … BARACK … OBAMA

Kweku

The Economy

The economy … is in a 'shamble'
That cannot wait … for 'transition'
Some think what's needed … is a bold 'gamble'
A 'blue' and a 'red' … 'position'

Not 'cured' … the economy 'affliction'
Awaiting a plan … to exact
Can Barack impede … the 'quick attrition'?
Before … the 'transitional act'

Pundits state views … without hesitancy
The economy … much too slow
Some suggest … a 'dual presidency'
To help … the economy grow

'Calls' for Barack's … economic vision
'Put into play' … at this moment
With George Bush … a 'concerted decision'
To share tactics … that are cogent

Many are anxious … to get something done
Economic circumstance … dire
Soon Obama … will be 'under the gun'
Along with his 'incoming … choir'

Kweku

Getting Started

Recession made worse ... by a 'credit crunch'
Finds corporations ... 'dejected'
Confident ... with a 'recovery punch'
Positive results ... expected

The most recent labor stats ... seem to 'state'
From last month ... a steady increase
A seven percent ... unemployment rate
For Barack ... somehow to 'decrease'

Barack laid out ... an 'economic scheme'
Two point five million jobs ... to 'glean'
Getting started ... is Barack's 'special team'
Jobs created ... are to be 'green'

Urgent action needed ... no time to waste
There is economic ... peril
Dire times that the country ... has seldom 'faced'
Awaiting results ... to herald

Economy ... deterioration
Is already ... on the 'table'
Ecology ... amelioration
Barack has plans ... to 'enable'

They seek to revive ... the economy
Deficit concerns ... have to 'wait'
They plan to respect ... the ecology
The environment ... they will 'sate'

In the country ... 'fiscal turmoil' is rife
'Main street' and 'Wall street' ... both confirm
Citizens ... demanding a 'better life'
'Turnaround' ... Obama's concern

The deficit solution ... is long term
It's disastrous ... to do so now
He plans an economy 'bump' ... that's firm
To the crisis ... he refuses to 'bow'

Eliminate programs ... we do not need
With the use ... of the proper 'wedge'
Will president elect Barack ... succeed?
With each 'repeated' ... campaign pledge

'Old' methodology ... needs 'new' mending
To do so ... Barack has a plan
His plan is to delete ... wasteful spending
True to his mantra ... 'yes we can'

With the 'economy' ... he is consumed
'Solution' ... needs all his 'cunning'
When the president's office ... is assumed
He plans to hit the ground ... 'running'

Kweku

Prongs In The Road

In 'race ills' ... will there be a 'reduction'?
Emphasizing ... its rejection
Will race no longer ... be a 'discussion'?
Due to Obama's ... election

Should Obama ... have a hectic 'first term'
That provokes ... national chagrin
Will 'race blindness' ... the nation 're-affirm'?
Or make race ... meaningful 'again'

Will 'ills of race' ... 'evaporate' away?
Departed ... the 'constant barrage'
Even with Barack ... is race here to stay?
Is 'departure' ... just a mirage?

Kweku

Chapter Six

Reflection

Into the mainstream ... has Barack 'blended'?
Easing centuries ... of chagrin
Obama's odyssey ... has not 'ended'
The 'voyage' is set ... to 'begin'

Eclectic Candidates

Not in any way ... should gender 'hinder'
To old thoughts ... none should be 'married'
Males and females ... were accenting gender
In 'new ways' ... candidates 'varied'

Race was a non issue ... but gender was
Some 'partisans' ... were heard to say
Many were upset ... with the 'gender buzz'
But the outcome ... they could not 'sway'

Must a God be chosen ... as 'THE FOREMAN'?
To wield ... the superior 'clout'
Christian ... Muslim ... or perhaps the Mormon
Should each claque ... in others have doubt?

An election ... for every 'season'
The candidates ... were eclectic
One's voting bent ... should not be deemed 'treason'
Constraints should be judged ... 'defective'

Is Barack Christian or Muslim ... some ask?
As though ... they disdain the latter?
For democracy ... a difficult 'task'
Have such choices ... never 'matter'

Kweku

Power Of The Press

To acknowledge … the power of the 'press'
A reality … not my 'goal'
Some 'black' as a 'black leader' … 'they' may 'bless'
The media's … much practiced role

Each black … a black celebrity must 'lead'
Just by … media volition
For whites … no white celebrity is 'keyed'
None is given … that 'position'

Now Obama … is president elect
What black leader … does he 'succeed'?
Barack … as a black leader … they 'reject'
All America … he must lead

Kweku

Aftermath

McCain 'closes in' ... on 'Barack's landslide'
The margin is small ... no ... it's vast
Support has divided ... no ... 'multiplied'
At that time ... no vote ... had been cast

As to Obama's ... political team
They seemed so much more ... energized
They presented to voters ... a 'plain theme'
Where the issues ... were emphasized

In 2009 ... a new 'resident'
A 4 year lease ... to the 'white house'
Barack Obama ... is the president
Now ... with national 'fires' ... to 'douse'

Obama and democrats ... won control
Despite veiled efforts ... to incite
Now there are republicans ... to console
Them to 'change' ... will Barack 'invite'?

Of the campaign ... was Barack reflective?
Did he think ... some events insane?
Of the future ... will he be 'receptive'?
Will some of the rancor ... remain?

Is national unity ... in his range?
Is the president ... respected?
Is Barack a true proponent ... of change?
As he said ... before elected

In his quest for change … will Barack falter?
Him … will the electorate rue?
Or will blue and red states … Barack alter?
To reflect … the red … white and blue

Barack … the catalyst for change … we need
President … of the USA
Will change begin … with 'deliberate … speed'?
And continue … the same old way

His opponents … who sit 'across the aisle'
Clinging … to a different 'stand'
Although Barack … they may attempt to rile
Will he choose … to extend his hand?

President Barack … the first lady too
With precious children … to coddle
A nation's eyes … on each thing they pursue
A new paragon … to model

Is Barack Obama … the 'chosen one'?
As 'Barack backers' … have perceived
When Obama's presidency … is done
In Barack … will more have believed?

Kweku

Divine Intervention

His optimism … could not be repelled
He was confident … what would be
Optimism such as his … I withheld
I was more … *let us wait and see*

When hearing him … his words were 'lyrical'
Of 'hope' … each word seemed 'symbolic'
He quickly … predicted a 'miracle'
His 'positive beat' … 'systolic'

It's as though by 'change' … he was 'invaded'
Kudos on Barack … he would 'pin'
On so many things … he had seemed 'jaded'
But he was sure … Barack would win

With religion … he was never 'content'
Now … the word 'God' … he often 'used'
He 'knew' that Barack … had earned God's 'consent'
For Barack's 'win' … he was 'enthused'

About Barack … he could not say 'enough'
He 'knew' … Barack was 'sent' by God
For him the election … would not be 'tough'
Barack Obama … had God's 'nod'

'Released' from him … all his 'inner tension'
About Barack … he yearns to talk
Barack's win … was 'divine intervention'
At other reasons … he will 'balk'

"Never in life" … he had once 'repeated'
But for faith … he began to 'search'
Some old demons … he has now 'defeated'
And he lives his life … for his church

Kweku

Some Gone – None Forgotten!

Each ancestor ... was a 'voting partner'
Without ... an alternative plea

Ancestors seemed to have ... the same 'charter'
On Barack ... 'each booth' did agree

The Voting Partner

In the past … each black … a big investor
Each ancestor … blacks still denote
There … in the voting booth … each ancestor
As though … they were casting a vote

Each ancestor … was a 'voting partner'
Without … an alternative plea
Ancestors seemed to have … the same 'charter'
On Barack … 'each booth' did agree

For each right … the ancestors were denied
And every minute … of fear
In the booth with pride … each vote was applied
And more than a few … shed a tear

Kweku

The Yam And The Soil

Parents pray ... there is nothing to 'restrict'
Potential ... though not evident
Few families ... are able to 'predict'
That their child ... will be 'president'

Parents may be subtle ... sometimes clever
Their 'choices' ... may be 'resonant'
But the child may choose ... the child's endeavor
Perhaps to be ... a president

A child's desire ... may not be 'evident'
This choice or that choice ... may have 'whirled'
But the child may want ... to be 'president'
And the leader ... of the free world

His life began ... with his dad's Kenyan 'root'
And a Kansas woman ... 'mixture'
The two produced ... an 'American fruit'
Now a presidential ... 'fixture'

'Simply' put ... that's Obama's genesis
And he to his own dreams ... adhered
To him ... will the world now be 'generous'?
As president elect ... 'revered'

Whether planned or not ... perhaps it's karma
That has brought us ... to where we are
Thank all the ancestors ... and Obama
It seems that we ... have come so far

When the 'yam' grows well … it may be the 'soil'
To the yam … credit may be due …
The yam did grow well … thank the soil and moil
And a president … did ensue

Kweku

The Sunday After

'This' is a day ... I thought never to see
Old and young ... at church repeated
More ecstatic... how could any day be
The sentiment ... seemed 'depleted'

Many foresaw the future ... by the past
'The Past' ... taught them what to expect
Each 'future prediction' ... 'in stone' seemed 'cast'
The 'except' ... now showed its 'effect'

For those in church ... they had 'faith' redefined
'Future' took on ... another 'look'
With faith in change ... they were 'there' now 'aligned'
The past and future ... they could 'brook'

Now ... faith is the substance of things ... hoped for
Amid the evidence ... of things not seen
Inside them ... that passage ... began to 'stir'
From the election ... 'faith' ... to glean

Barack Obama ... is not a 'cure all'
The preacher ... seemed to emphasize
On Obama ... all the weight should not 'fall'
'Ills' from us ... we must exorcise

Kweku

SAY WHAT?

A statement one makes ... may 'raise' an eyebrow
And the words become ... 'food for thought'

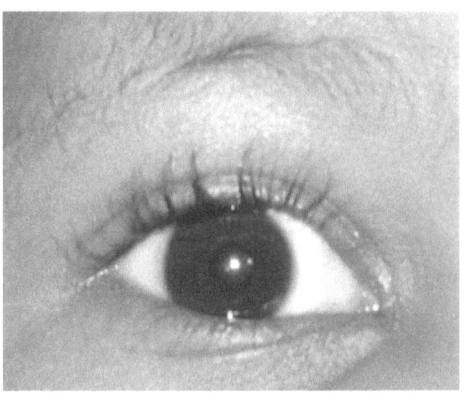

Another may question ... on 'when' and 'how'
Now aware ... of what 'change' has wrought

WHEN AND HOW?

Raising An Eye-Brow

A 'story' you tell kids ... think 'when and how'
Kids believe ... such days never were
Your 'memory bank' ... may raise an eye-brow
Feigned 'disbelief' ... may then recur

Quite carefully ... an example you 'pick'
At your words ... children show surprise
But still to your premise ... you choose to 'stick'
What comes next ... children can't surmise

Sitting and talking ... you summon your spouse
You both lament ... on 'days long gone'
At one time ... there was no phone in the house
Now ... kids have cell phones ... of their own

From the children ... comes more feigned 'disbelief'
That mom and dad ... survived such 'woes'
Yet with the children ... is a great relief
That 'their days' ... have not been like 'those'

Again you laugh ... hearing a 'foreign ting'
That reinforces ... what you said
One child 'picks up' ... since it's their 'cell phone ring'
Not an 'old ring' ... that's 'land line bred'

Now laughter ... 'sparks' more examples to cite
More phenomena ... to 'debate'
Infectious laughter ... examples invite
But to progress ... they all relate

At one time ... there was no black president
No black ... secretary of state
To laugh at that ... children were 'reticent'
It seemed to that ... they could 'relate'

Cheerfully ... all the children choose to sit
Each 'statement' given ... they explore
'Stories' of the past ... make them think a bit
Questions from them ... begin to 'pour'

Kweku

President 2044?

Will Barack's 'run' ... be a first testament?
A preview ... of what will ensue

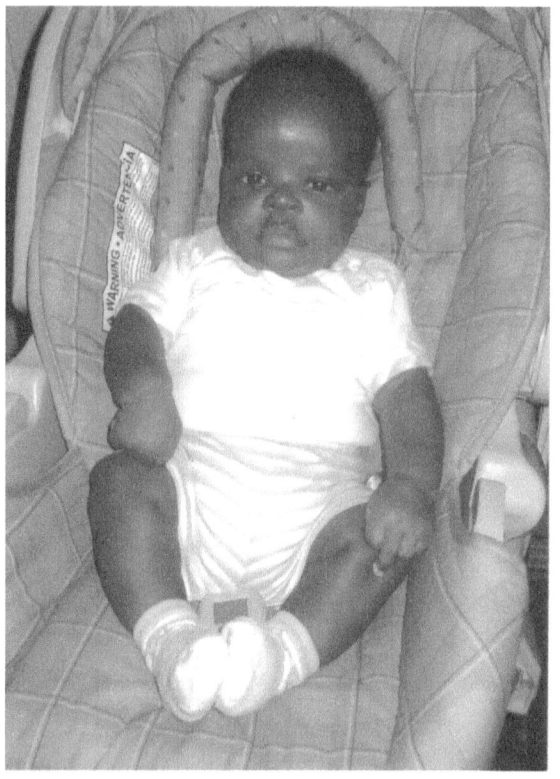

Will Barack be ... just the first president?
With much more ... than a tinge of hue

A DREAM PREFERRED

President 2044?

Will the 'second' … each of us live to see?
And will male or female … matter?

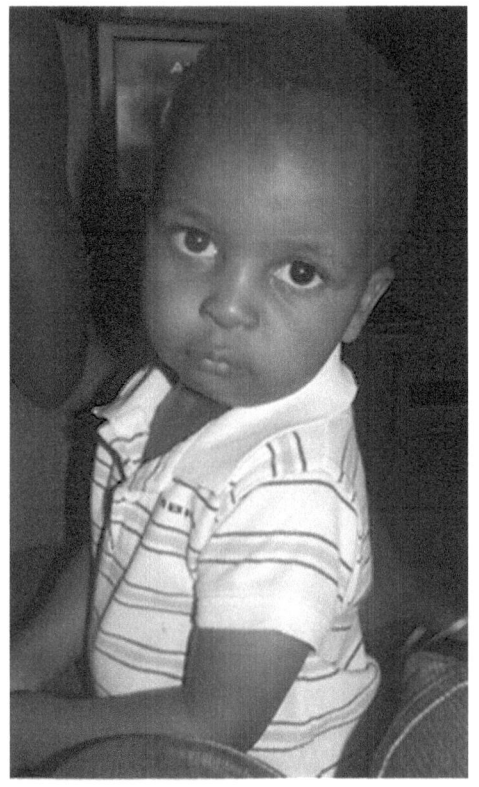

A 'democrat' … or perhaps 'GOP'?
Could it truly be … the 'latter'?

MUST MY FEMININE DREAMS …
REMAIN DEFERRED?

A Preview

A live preview ... 'on-going attraction'
Obama's ... presidency 'run'
Amid each trite ... 'personal distraction'
Can a 'terrorist' ... get 'it' done?

Will Barack's 'run' ... be a first testament?
A preview ... of what will ensue
Will Barack be ... just the first president?
With much more ... than a tinge of hue

Kweku

Prospect

November 4th ... brought a 'picture' of glee
The day ... the voters had spoken
Many others are pleased ... with those like me
Barack ... will not be a 'token'

He is not ... to sit 'idly' at the 'stairs'
As a 'figurehead' ... neglected
The national leader's 'mantle' ... he 'wears'
His solutions ... are expected

Barack ... the Executive elected
For his office ... he displays 'vim'
Other candidates ... have been 'rejected'
Now it is only ... 'up to him'

'Affirmative Action' ... sure to 'arise'
Should the program ... be abolished?
Solutions his team ... may have to 'apprise'
Since Barack ... has been 'acknowledged'

For 'their' solutions ... people now implore
On Barack ... the leadership 'falls'
The country's image ... he has to 'restore'
Although some ... his 'position' galls

His 'first move' ... may provoke dichotomy
'Political ... heredity'
Perhaps ... something on the economy
He may think ... a 'necessity'

'Inertia' … now thought of as 'cruel'
A problem … of 'delinquency'
Known issues … on alternative fuel
And foreign oil … dependency

Still to be caught … the reviled Osama
Epitomizing … all the 'worst'
Will he get captured … 'under' Obama?
Allaying those … Osama 'cursed'

Iran … Iraq … North Korea … and more
The Middle East … and Pakistan
'All' … are problems … for Barack … to explore
Russia … China … Afghanistan

Will he wait … until inauguration?
And delay … some future chagrin
Does he now engage … 'in conversation'?
Are plans getting made … to 'begin'?

To be expected … is the 'sober day'
Those are the days … for which he yearned
'President' … is more than a 'sobriquet'
'President' Obama … has earned

Kennedy's 'New Frontier' … 're-asked again'
What for the country … can you do?
Barack's 'Hope Over Fear' … 'tasked to begin'
'Change To Believe In' … to pursue

On Obama's 'plate' … is a 'heavy meal'
For 'dinner' … he cannot come late
Now in control … of the 'president's seal'
Many expect him … to be 'great'

Kweku

96

On Lies

A lie by any name … is but a lie
Other 'lives' … a lie may effect
The lies on which … 'politicians' rely
Require a method … to detect

For politics … there is 'change' that I need
A change … that rates 'high' on my list
'Lie usage' … seems motivated by greed
And needs of the voter … are 'missed'

Are there ways … to eliminate the lie?
What of a new … lie detector?
On my list … that invention would rate 'high'
Name it … a 'Voter Protector'

In 'truth serum' … he or she is 'immersed'
Each time … a politician lies
And the opponent … will be 'reimbursed'
For each lie … the 'liar' denies

A 'Lying Quotient' … voters can measure
Perhaps label it … an 'LQ'
A 'voter treasure' … that brings great pleasure
And more lies … voters may eschew

Will both sides of the aisle … need 'surgery'?
To repair … the status quo 'boat'
Can each 'campaign lie' … become 'perjury'?
Enacted … 'Impeding the Vote'

Let us also include … the 'Robo Call'
Test it … under our 'scrutiny'
The political lies … let's 'trap' them all
And call 'it' … 'Voter Mutiny'

Will lies continue to be … expected?
Hard for politicians … to spurn
Will 'Voter Protectors' … get 'rejected'?
Both sides of the aisle … 'overturn'

Kweku

Not Yet

Obama's election ... brings 'end' to race
A concept ... hoped for and believed
After the election ... I saw a 'trace'
Of race ... 'previously' perceived

Bill Bennett ... conservative 'referent'
On the election ... did react
Race no longer ... achievement 'detriment'
Barack's election ... did 'redact'

On television ... a known 'phone in show'
Topic ... 'general election'
'Disgust with Barack' ... calls began to 'grow'
In racial ways ... their 'dejection'

November 5th ... 'one' woke up 'socialist'
Knowing Barack's ... 'cabinet plan'
She said her country ... was at 'social risk'
Barack ... Ayers ... Wright ... and Farrakhan

Off brick walls ... logic began to 'career'
Each accusation ... was 'loaded'
Barack was slow ... at the voting machine
Just in Kenya ... had he voted

Barack is not ... a U. S. citizen
His presidency ... is a ploy
In some 'Arab place' ... he's a denizen
The U. S. ... he means to destroy

The 'code' ... I stopped trying to 'decipher'
At allegations ... I would scoff
To me ... the callers seemed ... much too 'hyper'
My television ... I turned 'off'

Despite Barack ... race is still a cancer
On old attitudes ... some are 'set'
His election is not ... the whole answer
Just maybe ... we are not 'there' yet

Kweku

Enigmatic Optimism

Do politicians mean the things ... they say?
Are words of rancor ... just a 'hoax'?
Will politics always get done ... that way?
Do voters 'agree' ... with their 'jokes'?

One accepted ... the other's concession
Is such an 'effort' ... just a 'sike'?
Will one of them ... offer a 'confession'?
The other ... he will never 'like'

Obama's ... long awaited 'ascension'
To the presidency ... 'unfurled'
Now he receives ... the greatest 'attention'
As the leader ... of the free world

There were those who worked ... for that 'prevention'
The 'negatives' ... they 'imparted'
'Today' ... are they 'immersed' ... in 'pretension'?
With negatives ... all 'discarded'?

Is national unity ... the new urge?
A process ... quickly to begin?
Will most accept ... a nonpartisan 'surge'?
Or their 'party' ... will most defend'?

Is there a sanctioned end ... to the 'race mess'?
The first scene ... of a new 'drama'
Is distrust gone ... with its constant duress?
Do we thank ... Mr. Obama?

Kweku

Pre-Transition

There are 'cries' for help … from the 'Wall Street Guy'
A loan … 'Auto Giants' request
For the 'Main Street Guy's' help … who will reply?
Some ask … who in 'them' will 'invest'?

There are times when 'Main Street' … may need a loan
Is government help … on the way?
Can 'Main Street' expect help … or stand alone?
In 'help' … will 'Wall Street' also 'play'

Some say it's too intricate … to explain
The government must do … its 'share'
With unanswered doubts … 'Main Street' may complain
Isn't corporate help … 'welfare'?

To some in America … a 'hero'
With Muslims … some 'positive bites'
But to Al Qaeda … just a 'House Negro'
Barack … does the bidding of 'whites'

Al Qaeda's 'play' … he understood fully
Nothing … would Al Qaeda 'redact'
Obama … they attempted to 'bully'
Barack was coy … did not react

The 'office' … Barack has not yet assumed
But issues … continue to 'mount'
With transition … he cannot be 'consumed'
For each issue … he must 'account'

Kweku

Cold Turkey

'Channel hopping' ... was their 'craved' depiction
By the coverage ... none were 'drained'
To the campaign ... some had an 'addiction'
An addiction ... that has not 'waned'

When will the next candidate ... 'possess' hue?
From the question ... so few refrained
Nothing definitive ... came as a 'clue'
Some uncertainty ... still remained

Will the 'second' ... each of us live to see?
And will male or female ... matter?
A 'democrat' ... or perhaps 'GOP'?
Could it truly be ... the 'latter'?

Can both parties ... have a person of hue?
One running against ... the other
Vile attacks on one ... will the other 'spew'?
While thrown right back ... is 'another'

Will either 'foe' see vile attacks ... as 'strange'?
With such a concept ... will they 'stay'?
Will they recall ... the politics of 'change'?
Will such be relevant ... 'that day'?

Complacent ... the voters refuse to be
Barack is not ... the 'last inning'
More good candidates with hue ... they will see
Barack is just ... the 'beginning'

Kweku

103

Anticipation

Is Obama's win … 'ratification'?
Old strategies … to defeat
Does Obama bring … anticipation?
A new claim … to 'global elite'

Kweku

Chapter Seven

Reality And Cabinet Building

My bent toward Barack ... was open and clear
Though my 'look' ... resembled the sphinx
Predictions he would win ... I did not 'cheer'
Since him I did not ... want to 'jinx'

So many said ... that I lacked 'confidence'
My persona ... was always grim
For me however ... ... it was 'common sense'
To never 'climb out' ... on that 'limb'

Still hard to believe ... but it must be true
The 'presidential seat' ... is filled
A world wide agenda ... he must pursue
First a cabinet ... he must build

Predicting & Fretting

Barack has not taken … the 'office oath'
But still demonstrates… he's 'in charge'
Pundit conjecture … continues in 'growth'
Senate confirmations … loom 'large'

The pundits are 'predicting' … and 'fretting'
On cabinet composition
While Obama's team … is busy 'vetting'
The cabinet competition

Hillary … his Secretary of State
'Hot topic' … on the rumor mill
Defense Secretary … still Robert Gates
A republican … 'on the hill'

Tim Geitner … Secretary of Treasure
Bill Richardson … to head 'Commerce'
In the stock market … an upward 'measure'
'Leakers' have been heard … to converse

Pundits … 'leakers' … buttressing a 'penchant'
A 'Homeland Security' 'claim'
For that job … pundits have often 'mentioned'
Janet Napolitano's name

For those of hue … another 'pinnacle'
Some say … a valid 'depiction'
Eric Holder … 'Attorney General'
More likely than not … 'prediction'

Of other appointments … rumors are rife
Tom Daschle … quite likely for 'Health'
For 'Agriculture' … Tom Vilsack has 'life'
A definite … lacking in 'stealth'

Some see the cabinet … so configured
As such … rumored to be 'pre-set'
But are all of them … being considered?
Without a decision … as yet

Many rumors … for a cabinet slot
But at times … the pundits are 'tricked'
History will 'render' … kudos or 'blot'
But only for those … who are 'picked'

Pundits and voters … take part in a 'game'
In which they have … 'cabinet voice'
But validated … is another 'claim'
That 'voice' must be … Obama's choice

Whether a 'leak' … or 'guess' … not yet confirmed
Certainly what has been … 'supposed'
For one result … Obama … is concerned
To get his cabinet … 'composed'

Kweku